unhurried
at work

Johnnie Moore

© Johnnie Moore 2020

All rights reserved. No part of this publication may be reproduced, stored in a retrieval system, or transmitted in any form or by any means, electronic, mechanical, photocopying, recording or otherwise, without the prior permission in writing of the publisher, except in the case of brief quotations embodied in a book review.

ISBN: 9798631556539

Contents

Introduction iii
   So what is unhurried? iii
   About this book iii
   How I began this journey iv

Part One: A hundred unhurried conversations 1
   What is an unhurried conversation? 3
   People are not blank slates 4
   People connect from where they are 5
   The magic is in the people 6
   There's more connection in struggles than success 7
   We're naturally good at listening 8
   Listening as a team sport 9
   Keeping it simple 10
   Tiny tweaks and sensitivities 11
   The joy of rambling 12
   What if someone never stops talking? 14
   Deeper structures below the surface 15
   Waiting with anticipation 16
   We are enough 17
   Hostages, volunteers and a Scandanavian surprise 18

Part Two: The unhurried path 21
   The wrong speed 23
   The subtle craft of turn-taking 24
   Rhythms and pendulums 26
   The wrong kind of simplicity 28

Not seeing the roots for the trees 31
Conformity 32
Falling in love with our stories 34
Dispelling horcruxes 36
Nothing is really stuck 38
Butterflies everywhere 39
Emotional debt and the Law of Ruts 40
We're in a mesh, not a mess 42
The possibility in impossibility 43
Ease into difficulty 44
Play with reluctance 46
Seek difference 48
Boredom. Gateway to the south! 49
Frustration is your friend 52
Learning is better than winning 54
Getting over ourselves 56
The spatula game and the teaching trance 60
Create agency 62
Moments 63
Practice 67
Despondent yoga 70
Start anywhere 71
Notes and Thanks 72

Introduction

So what is unhurried?

Unhurried is about us all doing the things that humans do best, the things that can't be replaced by machines and algorithms. It's about finding a way of working that counters the pressures of an always-on world.

It's about building more satisfying connections so that we can spend less of our time consuming energy and resources that are running out.

Unhurried doesn't always mean slow. It's more about moving at the right pace for the task at hand. When we're working with others, unhurried is not always going as fast as the most impatient person in the room.

It's also about accepting ourselves as we are: messy, imperfect, *normal* human beings. Funnily enough, this willingness to accept our ordinariness is what sometimes makes magic happen.

About this book

In this book, I begin by reflecting on a series of unhurried conversations I've run in the last few years. They use a simple format to change the pace at which we talk, and I've run them online, in my home city of Cambridge and around the world – and others host them as far afield as Santa Cruz and Bangalore.

Then I share some of the ways I think this emerging practice I call unhurried can be applied to the rest of our lives. Much of this book draws on material I've written in blog posts over the last few years working as a facilitator.

Feel free to read the pages in any order, I've designed this book for dipping in and out.

How I began this journey

I love improv theatre.

I love the games improv actors play to build their craft. And I especially love a great show where it's hard to believe the performers could connect so brilliantly without any script.

But the last show I'd been in had been excruciating. The scenes were awkward, the actors tripped over each other's lines. And the plot became absurd. There was a kind of laughter in the audience, but it was awkward and not heartfelt. A scene that started as a simple meeting of two decorators at a funeral home turned into a trip to Mars on marshmallow motorbikes. It was all the more painful that I was one of the performers.

My friend Antony and I were discussing it the next day. I'll never forget the conversation.

He said he realised that the difference between great improv and terrible improv was simple. The good shows, he said, were *unhurried*.

It was a throwaway line. But to me it felt like a real insight, not just about improv theatre, but about a lot of things in our daily lives.

After that conversation, I found myself using "unhurried" more and more when talking about what I wanted. It gradually became a kind of touchstone for me.

I didn't know when I started down this path just how far it would take me over the next five years.

∼

Part One:
A hundred unhurried conversations

It started with frustration.

I kept going to exasperating networking events. It felt like everyone there was trying to sell and no-one seemed to be buying. So there was a lot of noise being made but no one was really being heard. And I suspect everyone was trying to sound confident and there was no space to share our struggles.

Much of the time, what I saw playing out were power games, individuals jockeying for position and dominance, sometimes consciously but often without really being aware of it.

When people compete for attention, they tend to think, act, and form judgements with a focus on surface appearances. It's those who are quickest on the draw that can seem the most impressive. People associate speed with efficiency and mistake it for effectiveness. So much energy is expended on "display", on winning or maintaining the alpha role, that we don't see how unproductive we become.

So one day, I decided to offer something different.

I called it an Unhurried Conversation. And my friend Antony and I started running them in a café in Cambridge, where we both live.

To begin with, it was sometimes just the two of us, sometimes a few more. But gradually word got around and more people started coming. Nowadays attendance can range from four or five all the way up to twenty. Friends have since picked up on the idea and are now offering these conversations in different places around the world.

What started as an experiment has turned into a practice, and I've now hosted well over a hundred of them.

What is an unhurried conversation?

An unhurried conversation uses a simple process to allow people to take it in turns to speak without being interrupted. Everyone agrees at the start that only the person holding a chosen object (often a sugar bowl) is allowed to talk. Once the speaker has finished, they put the object down, signalling that they have said what they want to say. Someone else then picks up the object and takes their turn. Each speaker can respond to some or all of what the previous speaker said, or they can take the conversation in an entirely new direction.

(In the online version, everyone chooses their own everyday object to use as the talking piece. They show it to their camera to signal starting and finishing and we keep to the principle of one person talking at a time.)

I normally run unhurried conversations online or in a café, open to any member of the public who wants to join. By not limiting the practice to certain groups or types, I've been able to listen to a wide cross-section of people. I've found that the more variety there is in the voices speaking and the experiences lying behind the words, the more there is to learn.

Each conversation has led to subtly different results, but they have all helped me understand how people connect when they are given the time and space to say what they want.

Here are a few of the things these conversations have taught me.

∼

People are not blank slates

The conversations I've taken part in are a constant reminder of the richness and variety of human experience. I've been lucky enough to hear an incredible range of stories from an incredible range of people: the retired serviceman managing his relationships with multiple girlfriends; parents dealing with the crises facing their adolescent children; hilarious stories of dating triumphs and disasters; shared experiences of victory and loss.

Listening to people speaking freely about themselves has helped remind me of something that, despite its simplicity, can easily be forgotten. The people we interact with don't appear out of thin air as blank slates, ready to be sculpted and created afresh. They aren't generic "human units" who respond in identical ways. Instead, they arrive with rich and complex life experiences that shape how they react to what others say and do. If we see them simply as resources in need of direction, we can miss much of the experience they can contribute.

People connect from where they are

When people talk openly and share the things that are meaningful to them – moments of joy or pain, cherished ideas, difficult memories – they open a channel or pathway to the listener. Insights into other people's experiences of life's struggles and adventures help us to connect with one another by giving us ways into each other's minds. At the same time, we can connect through sharing the apparently mundane experiences we have in common, finding a resonance with each other in a shared perspective.

In business environments, it's tempting to obsess about the future. There are targets to be hit, growth levels to be reached, results to be achieved. But when we get too tangled up with what *might* happen, or what we *want* to happen, we can lose sight of the fact that the people we interact with are where they are *now*. The only way we can connect meaningfully is by understanding that our interactions take place in this moment. We have to be present *here*, not caught up in our plans for the future.

The magic is in the people

This method is as ancient as human civilisation itself. In many traditional cultures, the item held by the speaker is an impressive ritual object with intricate carving or inlays that signify the solemn duties of the speaker. In my updated version, I deliberately choose a much more mundane object, like a sugar bowl or pepperpot. This feels less solemn, and is also intended to avoid the idea that the magic lies in an object when really it's in the people sitting together.

We've probably all heard the mantra that we should "trust the process" but I prefer to trust the people. Much as I enjoy unhurried conversations following the principles described here, there's nothing sacrosanct about the process and I don't suggest it as a miracle cure. When I run a conversation, I don't try to enforce the 'unhurried rules' very strictly. In the end it's a **practice** – something you do in order to see what you can learn, not a **procedure** to follow regardless of what happens around you.

There's more connection in struggles than success

I remember one particularly satisfying conversation I hosted for a big team of people who were participants on a leadership course. I went into the conversation feeling anxious. Would these folks be tempted to play high status and talk in the abstract about good leadership?

I needn't have worried. The first person to talk shared his grief at a recent bereavement and took his time. What followed was a series of very personal stories of the struggles people in the room were facing.

This wasn't an entirely new phenomenon, but it was the moment when something became crystal clear to me: Stories of success, especially individual success, easily become isolating. We connect much more deeply when we openly share our struggles and risk vulnerability.

∼

We're naturally good at listening

Many of us have been trained to be "**active**" listeners. In practice, this easily turns us into **hyperactive** listeners: we nod vigorously and affirm the speaker but these gestures often feel like a coded way of saying, "hurry up, it's my turn next".

In the right circumstances, though, listening is easy. First timers in unhurried conversations are often surprised at how well they manage to just listen to others. It turns out we're better listeners than we think.

Letting a speaker say what they want without rushing them or cutting them off if they go "off script" creates an environment in which ideas can flow freely. There is a common assumption that conversations will somehow end badly if we don't "stick to the topic". But with patient listening, we often discover that contributions which might, at first, seem to be "off topic" are, in fact, connected. What's important is that we trust the speaker and listen sympathetically to help find these connections.

In a normal conversation, we can easily find ourselves waiting anxiously for the place where we can interrupt to have our say. We can spend a lot of energy maintaining that alertness. Funnily enough, when the structure closes off that option it's actually easier to relax and just listen.

Listening as a team sport

When there are several listeners for each speaker, we can all relax a bit as the work of listening is shared. Instead of having to hang on every word, we can allow our minds to wander a little and free up the space to respond imaginatively, speaking as we wish rather than as we've been conditioned to think we should.

This doesn't mean cutting our connection with the speaker and ignoring them. So long as we're sensitive to what else is going on around us, and so long as we're ready to do our part when needed, we can let the group as a whole carry the conversation forward.

In a meeting, just as in a group conversation, it can be useful to take a mental step back for a while. There's no shame in taking the time to explore your own thoughts, flesh out a new idea, or frame a detailed response to a point. The fact that someone is speaking shouldn't be a straitjacket that prevents someone else from daydreaming. When people listen as a group, you can feel a sense of connection – and rather like in a sports team, people can fulfil different roles.

∼

Keeping it simple

People are often puzzled, and sometimes even slightly alarmed, when I tell them that most unhurried conversations are run without a theme. The idea that we can gain a lot from simply asking others to share whatever is on their mind can seem counterintuitive when we're used to more rigid structures. I am constantly surprised by what happens in an unhurried conversation, and you might be too.

The simplest structures often free people to do the most complex things. When we minimise the rules that govern a conversation, we open up the space for ideas to flourish and connections to form without constraints.

When kicking off a public conversation, I keep things short and simple. Even if there are some basic rules and principles to follow, I've learned that these things usually take care of themselves. Confidentiality, for example, can be important when speaking in public. However, we don't normally talk about it in advance as we've found that people implicitly understand how to keep themselves safe in this kind of space. By making the rules light, and only intervening if necessary, we foster a space in which speakers have the freedom to explore boundaries by themselves without having to fit into a predetermined template.

This is why I don't include a suggestion to people that they should "speak from the heart". This is often a feature of the talking-stick processes on which unhurried conversations are based, and it's fine in many contexts. But I think it can be counter-productive, making people self-conscious and self-censoring.

Tiny tweaks and sensitivities

One of the little pleasures of doing something so many times is that you notice tiny details.

There's a little dance in the way people take and hold the talking object. Some clutch it to their breast, others hold it out at arms length as if it holds secret power, others again simply park it in front of them, merely nudging it forward a couple of inches to indicate when they've finished.

The size and shape of furniture seems to affect the conversation in subtle ways. Sitting around a big table produces longer silences a lot of the time. Lower, smaller tables often seem to go with a lighter and faster pace. I held a conversation recently in a room without tables, so we put the object on the floor. This was a longer variation of the process with a break in the middle. The first half seemed a little cautious compared to usual. In the break, I found some cushions and raised the object a few inches off the ground, so that people looking at it were nearer to having eye contact with each other. This seemed to raise the energy in part two.

If you try the process yourself, your mileage will surely vary, as does mine. I've learnt that there aren't clear rules to this, and it's fun to be aware of the tiny sensitivities that colour the conversation.

The joy of rambling

Some of the best conversations take place when we roam around many different topics, allowing ourselves to move from one to another as the mood takes us.

Because I usually don't set a theme in an unhurried conversation, the topics can bounce from intense international politics one minute, to someone's personal story about their home life the next. Because we aren't trapped by what has gone before, we can more easily cope with shifts of mood from light to deep, from joyous to fierce to tearful.

Understanding that we don't have to immediately come up with a thoughtful and significant response to the previous speaker gives us the room to tackle issues in our own time. It can defuse tensions and conflicts.

When we try to constrain an interaction to a predetermined outcome, we believe we are being efficient. And sometimes we are. Certain types of meetings, like briefings or progress reports, benefit from shared expectations about structure and flow. But when we meet to exchange and develop ideas, agendas can blind us to a lot of what is going on. This means we can miss out on a lot of the potential available to us.

So in the unhurried format, we don't have to worry about sticking to an agenda and laboriously connecting to what has come before. And at the end, we often realise that there are threads that weave the strands back together. We don't have to work hard at it … we can let it happen naturally.

One of my favourite conversations happened when we switched to a new café at the last moment. Someone started the conversation by observing that the teapots at the table had a really nice design. He shared his frustration with teapots that often seemed to drip. You might think this a rather trivial way to start a conversation. But what followed was a series of stories about design that slowly mutated from the design of crockery to the design and the purpose of our lives. We meandered between the light and the profound in a delightful way you couldn't possibly have planned. In contrast, I've sometimes participated in important sounding gatherings aiming for deep dialogue and found them fragmented and cranky. You can't force these things.

∽

What if someone never stops talking?

I usually include one piece of wisdom when I open an unhurried conversation. I say that if you're new to this, you might be sitting there worrying, "what if someone grabs the sugar bowl and talks for an hour and a half?" This nearly always gets a laugh, I guess because it names a real concern for newcomers. I usually then say something like this: "Well, that's never happened. But if it did, I'd probably decide this is a good chance to practice lowering my shoulders and relaxing. And imagining that I'd paid money to attend this remarkable theatrical monologue."

And in my experience, when people know they aren't going to be interrupted, and really are being listened-to, they are much less likely to ramble on. (I should add that a friend who has run these in Spain felt obliged to introduce a time-limit as his group seemed not to follow my experience. But better to add tiny pieces of structure only if you really need to.)

Deeper structures below the surface

There's a lot more going on when we talk to each other than just an exchange of information. There's a dance of conversation in which we viscerally respond to and reflect each other. Our thoughts and words collide, come together, leap off at tangents, and create patterns and meanings that are new and unique to the moment. There's far more happening when we talk than any transcript could hope to convey.

Many familiar group processes focus on generating explicit results – we want answers on post-it notes, ratings on evaluation forms, documented action plans. But when we devote all our attention to surface-level outcomes, we run the risk of missing the subtler connections that group dynamics can reveal.

Waiting with anticipation

Hosting so many of these meetings has led me to understand that people have an enormous capacity to share deeply and to uncover fascinating new connections without the need for clever probing questions from a leader.

My willingness to wait, sitting with silence and allowing the conversation to unfold on its own terms, has become far greater as a result of these experiences. I might still be anxious in those moments when everything seems to have come to a halt, and I might still worry that I'm expected to do something – *anything* – to keep the conversation moving. But I've learned that the ability to restrain myself, to resist the urge to nudge people along, can have profound results.

If we can bring ourselves to wait with anticipation, we create space for other people to generate ideas and insights of their own, rather than ones pre-formed by our expectations. Time and again, when I hold back from saying something clever to fill the silence, and wait patiently, the next person who speaks offers something much more interesting and surprising than I could have.

We are enough

People also find a lot of satisfaction in the simple experience of talking together. The unhurried approach invites us to work with who we already are. It doesn't involve a lot of consumption, beyond a cup of tea or coffee and perhaps a biscuit or two.

∼

Hostages, volunteers and a Scandanavian surprise

It's a feature of what I call the café version of unhurried conversations that everyone who turns up has come by invitation, with some idea of what they're signing up for. So they are already anticipating something a bit different when they arrive.

I sometimes use the process in my work with organisations, but it's a fine judgement as to whether to do so and when. In work meetings, people haven't volunteered so it's not quite the same. If the process feels too much like an uncomfortable imposition, then it won't work in a satisfying way. That said, some of the most amazing things have happened when I've used the process in a work context.

I have vivid memories of running a strategy day for a very diverse group of businesspeople from different countries, struggling to work out how to create a new sustainable partnership between their companies.

After a morning spent briefing each other, I chose to start the afternoon with an unhurried conversation – this time with a topic, the self-evident one of "how are we going to make this happen?" People were comfortable with the format so the conversation went on for quite a long time.

Then, just before we were due to take a tea break, one of the participants took his turn. We'll call him Sven. He was one of two representatives of a Scandinavian business with a big stake in the project. Very carefully and very politely, he said something like this:

"When I came to England this morning, I had very high hopes for this meeting. I greatly respect Frank (the chairman of this group) and this is clearly a very talented and committed group of people."

This sounded promising. What came next was more of a surprise. He continued in the same reasonable tone:

"But I have to admit, I am now disappointed. It does not sound as if we are really committed to making this happen, nor have we agreed on any realistic goals. I am not sure what we should do about this."

At which point he stopped, and I observed it was time to take a break.

I admit I was a bit concerned about what Sven had said, and several people approached me anxiously during the break hoping I would have a way to make things better. The break was quite short and as everyone sat down, I thought the best thing would be to not try to do anything *clever*. So I just continued the unhurried process to see what would happen.

The next thing, as it turned out, was that Sven's business partner grabbed the talking object and said something that was quite unexpected.

"Sven and I have decided to commit to investing 200,000 euros in the prototype of this product."

I don't know what had happened, but I'm guessing the two partners had chatted during the break and decided to take the initiative in addressing the concern they had raised. What might have been treated as a problem for me to solve with some clever process, had instead solved itself within this very simple one.

What followed were a series of offers from other participants to move the project on in a variety of unexpected ways.

Part Two:
The unhurried path

The more unhurried conversations I took part in, the more I realised that my own views were evolving. I didn't sit down after each session to dissect the conversations and analyse what I'd learnt. And I didn't approach the sessions with the goal of seeking out and pinning down some universal truth. But when I stopped to reflect on the experiences as they built one on top of another, I realised a pattern was emerging that pointed the way towards a broader practice and way of viewing the world.

I also realised that over five years of hosting them, I'd changed the way I was working in other parts of my life. I was more patient, more willing to sit with awkward silences. Meetings became more interesting and I felt more present to what was going on.

People are often excited about particular tools or methods for changing the outside world. Perhaps the most satisfying thing about unhurried is how much it has changed me.

The world is a complex place where simple actions have unintended consequences, and where misunderstanding, frustration and surprise are commonplace, not exceptional. Unhurried conversations feel like a way of flowing with, rather than fighting against, the network of constantly changing connections in which we are all embedded.

The practice of approaching people and problems in an unhurried way offers not so much a model as a ***rhythm*** for approaching life and its challenges.

I sometimes describe unhurried as the practice of recognising and accepting the entangled nature of the world we live in. It's about creating the time and space to work so that solutions can arise naturally. We can develop ways of thinking and interacting with others that are appropriate for the messy reality we live in.

In the rest of this book, I'm going to share some thoughts about how we might do that. Because this is a book, and one page inescapably follows the next, I've put these ideas into some form of linear order. But the truth is that they could be rearranged in all sorts of other ways. I suggest you browse them and read them in the order that appeals to you, finding your own connections and a flow through that fits your own ideas and experiences.

Rather like the threads of an unhurried conversation, you may find that regardless of the order in which you read them, and whether you read all of them or just a few, you'll make your own sense of them in the end.

The wrong speed

We live in impatient times.

We have been sold the idea that speed is an end in itself. Time is money, we hear, so we think that the faster something works, the more productive, efficient and intelligent it must be.

Apparently, a one-second delay in each customer loading up their webpage would cost Amazon $1.6 billion a year, so there's clearly not a second to be lost! Serving customers quickly brings down retail costs, so we mustn't let customers, or those serving them, dawdle.

Everywhere we turn, speed is king.

The danger is that we end up trying to run our brains at a pace more suited for computers than for humans. The fear of any sort of delay pushes us to make decisions and take actions that are driven by short-term perspectives. And as we are profoundly social creatures, that sense of panic becomes viral, and we infect each other with our haste and anxiety.

We need to find a pace that is better suited to us.

The subtle craft of turn-taking

In their book, *A General Theory of Love*,[1] Thomas Lewis, Fari Amini and Richard Lannon describe an experiment. A baby is playing with her mother, exchanging looks and gestures and smiles. This is happening over a high-quality video link, but the level of engagement seems like it's face-to-face.

Then the experimenters introduce a two-second delay in the video feed. Quite suddenly, the child moves from contentment to distress. Just a small disruption of the synchrony has remarkable consequences. It disrupts the baby's sense of connection and safety.

As a friend of mine puts it, babies are born understanding the subtleties of turn taking – you go, then I go.

Too often we're not good at taking turns; we interrupt and rush each other, actions that come with a significant emotional cost.

We easily miss the value of small interactions with other human beings, something that's accentuated by our use of devices. We use selfie sticks so we don't have to ask others to take our pictures. We use Google maps, so we don't need to ask the locals for directions. Go into a post office or shop or train station and you might see a crowd of people, all interacting with machines but not really acknowledging each other.

These devices appear to save us time, but they may be depriving us of a stronger, more primal sense of connection.

Professor Elizabeth Stokoe spends her life analysing conversations in minute detail. There's a whole academic field devoted to the process, meticulously annotating conversations down to each um, err and change of stress. Her book, *Talk, the Science of Conversation*,[2] is full of examples of the impact of tiny, easily overlooked fragments of conversations. She explains how, when two friends speak on the phone, they say a variation of "hi" to each other six or seven times. It's only when they feel they have synced up that they proceed to the rest of the conversation. If you think conversations are about information exchange, this might seem inefficient, but it's profoundly human.

∼

Rhythms and pendulums

There is a lot going on when people talk. Much of the deeper meaning can go unnoticed.

We humans are sensitive to our environments. Our brains absorb and process far more information than we can consciously attend to, because if we focused on every tick of the clock, every shadow on the floor, every spatial relation between each item on the table, we would be overwhelmed by the assault of raw information.

It's impossible to analyse and absorb every little meaningful detail in this web of interaction and communication. But we don't need to. Through patient listening and an openness to events around us, it's possible to fall in with the patterns of non-verbal communication.

When you mount two or more pendulums on a platform together, swinging at different speeds, they will eventually, as if by magic, begin swinging together in the same rhythm. This happens because almost imperceptible vibrations are passed from one to another through the platform, gently nudging each towards the others a fraction at a time. Without any outside interference, they begin to align with each other. The magic comes from the fact that the environment itself works as a passive means of transferring information. I sometimes think something like this happens in an unhurried conversation.

Communication is more than just a matter of saying the right things and articulating our thoughts in the most precise way. As the improvisation teacher, Viola Spolin, says, "Information is a very weak form of communication."

Our words, and just as much our silences, are notes and beats in a complex performance of improvised music that we play alongside dozens or hundreds of other musicians. To keep the music flowing, we have to sense how our own contributions fit and how best to give the other players the room they need to shine.

Incidentally, being in sync doesn't necessarily mean going slow all the time. Just slowing down a bad experience won't make it a good one. Unhurried is not always about going slowly. It's about finding a way to create resonance between us as we work.

If you watch a Formula 1 pit crew at its peak, it services a car incredibly fast. It succeeds because of practice and a collective alertness to the movements of individuals. What can look fast to an outsider can seem measured to a practiced insider.

∽

The wrong kind of simplicity

Many of our problems started life as solutions.

When we hurry, we look for shortcuts and reach for simple explanations to make sense of complex situations, too impatient and too fearful to take the time to think things through. And in doing so, we make the wrong kinds of simplifications about the world.

Simplifying problems and situations is a key part of the way humans think and make decisions. We group individuals together because it's easier to think about a handful of common characteristics than thousands of differences. We make maps and draw up models to help us cut through the noise and identify the essential features of an environment or problem. These help us manage the complexity in the world. But if we move too hastily, if we allow ourselves to be rushed by the need for quick results, then these tools can become traps.

Dietrich Dorner's *The Logic of Failure*[3] is a fascinating exploration of how this kind of simplification can lead to disaster. Dorner studied the approaches of many different people to identical computer simulations of complex real-world challenges, such as managing a drought-prone region of Africa. This data allowed him to identify the common patterns of behaviour that led most players to cause catastrophic droughts and crop failures, and to compare them with the minority who learned to manage the systems successfully.

Dorner discovered that one of the key reasons people fail to manage complex systems is that they move too quickly and rush to judgements: they diagnose a problem, identify a cause, and then immediately turn to implementing their solution. The problem is that initial attempts to simplify complex systems rarely take proper account of all the important variables. When people start from flawed or incomplete assumptions and get attached to rigid goals, swift implementation only serves to speed up a disastrous outcome.

Some participants in Dorner's experiment focused on reducing tsetse flies, for instance, with the goal of building up stronger cattle populations to feed the people of the region. But while this simple goal may have made intuitive sense, the unsustainable cattle growth that followed eventually caused a complete collapse of the finely balanced ecosystem. Other people focused on solving water shortages by drilling more wells. But while the wells provided short-term benefits, they ultimately caused ground water supplies to be exhausted, leading to drought.

What the unsuccessful people had in common was that they focused on simple fixes and missed the subtle signals giving feedback about the complexity of the system. They treated their initial simplified models as if they captured everything they needed to know and moved forward without testing their assumptions. To put it simply, they failed to notice.

The more successful participants understood that before they could set out for their destination they needed to first explore the landscape. Only then could they adjust their initial map until it provided a useful guide to the ground.

The key difference is that the successful managers understood that they were testing ideas, not deciding the truth of the matter. This meant they were more attentive to feedback and thus more willing to adapt their models and change their goals as they discovered more about the system.

By listening for new signals, and seeking out new information that might test and challenge our ideas, we can develop solutions progressively. Taking an unhurried approach to building our models doesn't mean that we move slowly – it means that we minimise our chances of getting lost quickly.

Not seeing the roots for the trees

The metaphor of the tree as an image for understanding systems has deep roots. The origins of Western systems of logic begin with the attempt to categorise the things in the world as belonging to classes that spread out and away from each other, like branches spreading out from a trunk. Items in the world are animate or inanimate – animate things are mortal or immortal – mortal animals are rational or irrational. Humans belong to the class of rational, mortal animals and are thus excluded from the irrational, immortal and inanimate branches of existence. As useful as this approach has been, it obscures the interconnections and ambiguities we see when we look at real individuals.

Ecologist Manuel Lima[4] has challenged the metaphor of trees and branches by inviting us to look more closely once again at the complex interconnectedness of natural systems. A tree-based model of species, for instance, creates clearly divided categories and encourages us to see the world as neatly carved up. But the reality is that individuals are not separated from each other, but inextricably intertwined. Humans are connected to their food sources, the world they live in, the bacteria in their gut, and it is their place in this mesh that makes them what they are. Indeed, scientists studying forests are uncovering how deeply interconnected even trees are, not above ground but in their intertwined roots below.

Conformity

Accepting the diversity of a culture can be scary. It means accepting that you can't just replicate yourself, your personality and your ideas in other people. You might be able to set the tone in some places to some extent, but there will always be networks, partnerships, interest groups and individuals that remain outside your control.

Back in the late 1980s, Michael Lewis wrote a book called *Liar's Poker*[5] about the way in which the great financial institutions of London and New York worked furiously to replicate their winning cultures. They hired "people like us" and then spent huge amounts of time and energy training those people further to "fit" the corporate identity. What Lewis noticed at the time was that this uniformity left these organisations blind to new data and viewpoints that didn't fit their predetermined view. He argued that this narrow vision would soon have catastrophic effects for the world financial system, as the companies just weren't able to see anything outside the bubble they created. Lewis was wrong about the timeframe but right about the ultimate result. 20 years later, his book *The Big Short* would document exactly how the refusal to see over the walls they had built brought many of these businesses to their knees.

When we work together in groups, we have a unique opportunity to pool our knowledge and the processing power of our brains in order to achieve more than we could if we worked alone. But communication in groups can be difficult. Cooperation is frequently undermined by fears, anxieties, power games, and pre-judgements about what other people want to hear.

In his article, *'Why Groups Fail to Share Information Effectively'*,[6] Jeremy Dean writes

> *Again and again [research] results have shown that people are unlikely to identify the best candidate, make the best investment or spot who really committed the crime. When asked to make a group decision, instead of sharing vital information known only to themselves, people tend to repeat information that everyone already knows.*

When we think about sharing a piece of new information with a group, we are often concerned that we'll be held responsible for it. If the information is wrong, we worry that people will think this is our fault. If what we say undermines someone else's suggestion, we think they might get angry at us. If the information is judged to be irrelevant, we'll look like we're just getting in the way. All sorts of prejudgements and anxieties can be obstacles to the honest exchange of information and ideas.

The underlying issue here is that communication is often treated as a competitive sport, with all sorts of points or social credits to be won or lost on the turn of a phrase. And when people compete, most are interested in coming away as the "winner".

If we want to make sure that people feel truly free to share, we need to make it easier to speak without recriminations, and for people to contribute with less pressure to conform to group expectations. That's much easier said than done, and that's partly why I often say unhurried is a practice, something we have to keep working at.

Falling in love with our stories

Thomas Cranmer was burnt at the stake for his beliefs. In his last moments, he thrust one hand into the flames. It was the hand that had signed the recantation of his beliefs, a recantation which he later dramatically reversed, leading to his execution. The image of his hand held into the flames is a vivid reminder of our willingness to suffer for our beliefs and our stories about the world. Sometimes, we might do better to be less convinced of the stories we tell ourselves.

There is strong research evidence that the specific techniques or schools of theory used in psychotherapy only have a relatively small impact on the ultimate outcome. What matters more are the unique circumstances of the client and the quality of their relationship with their therapist. Often, people are led to new ways of thinking and practice by synchronising with other people and ideas, rather than through the persuasive power of hard-edged intellectual frameworks. Explanations are popular because they can be gobbled up and "understood", but half a dozen different explanations can all get someone to exactly the same place in the end.

In *A General Theory of Love*, the authors write,

> *Patients are often hungry for explanations because they are used to thinking that neocortical contraptions like explication will help them. But insight is the popcorn of therapy. When patient and therapist go together, the irreducible reality of their mutual journey is the movie.*

Or as I sometimes put it, *relationships before ideas*.

People love doing quizzes that tell them what type of person they are because we love a simple explanation. Lots of patients are thrilled to get a diagnosis, even one that doesn't really fit, because having a label for their suffering is a relief in itself.

Human beings love storytelling and stories are one of the most powerful motors for inspiring people and giving them purpose. But sometimes we're too quick to assemble facts into stories and at other times we take the further step of becoming attached to these stories or insisting that they are the only "real" truth.

We've all got our own collection of wooden legs, stories we tell ourselves that might once have served a purpose but now act as limitations. Our stories are part of our self-identity. But what would happen if we invited in some creative doubt to soften our stories about who we are?

Once we start recognising narratives for what they are – stories that we can choose to accept or not – we can approach them more creatively. And when we see the narratives we've made for ourselves we regain some freedom, rather than letting stories we've told decide which paths we will take.

Dispelling horcruxes

In the Harry Potter series, the evil wizard Voldemort attempts to attain immortality by creating horcruxes. He splits off a fragment of his soul and stores it in an object or person so that he can be reconstituted from the horcrux in the event of his death. The terrible thing is that in his pursuit of immortality, Voldemort leads a cruel and miserable life, splintered and broken.

In the real world, we're often tempted to create something like horcruxes of our own. We take our ideas, our desires and our qualities, and we invest them in things like houses, cars, relationships, ideas and jobs. We don't notice that, by investing in them, we have, like Voldemort, split off a part of ourselves and given it away.

One of the biggest horcruxes I made for myself was a sports car. I was earning good money in advertising, which is a business that is all about the creation of horcruxes. Smoking my own dope, I imagined that if I bought this hot car I'd be driving to the French riviera every weekend, the sun beating down on my suddenly-more-attractive self as my colourful life unfolded in front of me.

When I *did* buy the car, what actually happened was that I slept very badly for three months, worrying that someone was going to scratch it outside my flat.

We can make horcruxes out of anything. I made one out of my car but you might make yours out of where you live, who you work for, or the person you've fallen in love with.

Part Two: The unhurried path

Harry Potter risked life and limb to destroy Voldemort's horcruxes. Maybe we can dispel our own a little more easily with a bit of awareness. No elder wand required.

∽

Nothing is really stuck

Everybody is dealing with how much of their own aliveness they can bear and how much they need to anesthetize themselves.
– Adam Phillips

It's a paradox of our hurried world that many of us feel stuck a lot of the time.

We find ourselves in our work and relationships going around in circles, frustrated with each other and seemingly doomed to fall into the same trap, again and again.

We feel stuck, but also furious – an interesting combination.

There's creative potential in the brew of emotion lying just below the rigid surface. This is where the real aliveness is. If we're brave enough to see it, we get a chance to bring our meetings, relationships – and ourselves – back to life.

Even a small shift in our attitude or behaviour can remind us that the system is not dead and stuck, but alive and possibly kicking. Just when a relationship, or an organisation, or a political situation seems irreversibly hopeless, I remind myself that nothing is really stuck.

Butterflies everywhere

Tending to the smaller details can have a huge effect on how things turn out in the bigger picture. Chaos theorists like to talk about the entanglement of scales, which means that large-scale outcomes in complex systems can't be separated from the small-scale events that take place in the same systems. Tiny changes can work their way up from the grassroots and have enormous effects on end results. This "sensitive dependence on initial conditions", better known as the "butterfly effect", helps explain why top-down heroic leadership styles can never provide the control that they promise. The reality is that small changes are big changes because they all form part of the same mesh.

But we easily end up competing with each other for big "strategic" insights. So the little shifts that might matter get disparaged. We sit at boardroom tables wringing our hands about high-sounding abstractions. The ability to hold these kinds of important conversations is often the route to power in organisations. But they easily distract us from the multiple, apparently mundane details that make up our real lives and may have more to do with how things really change.

∽

Emotional debt and the Law of Ruts

Our organisations sometimes seem stuck because of what I call **emotional debt**.

It's inspired by a thing computer programmers call "technical debt". By this they mean the ever-rising cost to a project of applying short-term fixes to their code without taking account of the bigger picture. Over time, these quick fixes compound with each other to make the overall software increasingly inefficient and hard to maintain.

We can easily see how similar processes apply to many projects outside programming. It's like constructing an improvised building in a haphazard way: as the building grows and develops it becomes increasingly unstable and more and more of the project's resources have to be expended on propping it up.

This is what happens when we rely on quick fixes in our working relationships. Teams tend to gloss over difficulties in how they relate – often because of the pressure of work but also because of the natural tendency to avoid having awkward conversations. By seeking ways around difficulties, teams tend to build up "emotional debt": the weight of unresolved questions, frustrations and past conflicts that reduce a team's ability to respond to challenges.

Emotional debt is often harder to pin down than technical debt: after a while, the limitations of sloppy code become fairly clear and the code itself is normally out in the open where everyone can see it and work on it. Emotional debt is normally hidden, and that makes it harder to deal with.

We often don't discover just how much emotional debt we've been carrying until some of it is resolved. I call this the Law of Ruts: you only realise how deep the rut has become when you finally step out of it. It's the classic moment when we look back and realise how we'd fallen under a spell from which we are now free.

∼

We're in a mesh, not a mess

When we're under stress, struggling with the pushes and pulls of conflicting priorities, demands, and deadlines, it can often seem like our lives are a mess. As we struggle to catch up, to make something happen, and to free ourselves from the pressures that weigh us down, we become like an animal caught in barbed wire.

I remember talking with a friend on a day we were both struggling with despondency bordering on despair. "Maybe I could just sell the house and move to France," he said. A little lightbulb went on for me as I recognised this attitude. It was something I did myself as well, but this time I was onto it. "That sounds like an escape fantasy," I said. Escape fantasies appear to offer us relief from our troubles, but are actually part of the deeper issue – the search for fast answers to tangled problems.

Perhaps if we take the time to relax into where we are now, we might find that the state we're in is a sign that we're not alone. We are entangled, enmeshed, inextricable from the wider world. Messiness and complexity are part of who we are. We aren't responsible for everything because the system acts on us just as we act on it. Being interdependent in this way is life itself. We're pulsating creatures, breathing in and breathing out. Acknowledging this might help us realise a different kind of power is available.

∽

The possibility in impossibility

Several years ago I was sitting in a Bangkok bar, severely exhausted. It was past midnight and I was huddled with eight emergency planning experts. It was the night before a three-day meeting to develop and implement a new system for managing natural disasters for an international aid agency.

As a team we'd already gone through a slew of anxious conversations about all the pitfalls you might expect to encounter at a conference hosting one hundred people from multiple cultures, many of whom would be using English as a second language. As facilitator for this event, I was the one most responsible for somehow seeing it through.

Eventually we acknowledged we'd done our best and there was nothing more we could do now. We all needed some sleep. The lead client, who I knew as a friend, turned to me and said, apologetically, "I'm sorry, we've made this impossible for you."

I found myself replying, "That's ok. If it wasn't impossible, I wouldn't be able to do it."

A sane life sometimes seems impossible but if we can embrace difficulty and be creative with chaos, we can start seeing them as allies rather than threats.

Ease into difficulty

Life's interesting challenges are inherently messy and confusing. Frustration, anxiety and all those other uncomfortable feelings are features, not bugs. They are part of the system and shouldn't just be shooed away by the imposition of a gleaming, perfect plan.

Instead of making things easy, what if we try to bring a sense of ease to things that normally provoke anxiety, urgency and over-reaction? Rather than running from challenges, what if we relax into them? By taking our time and slowing down a little, we can explore the problem more deeply rather than rushing into the easiest 'solution'.

Many times while writing this book, I have stared at my screen in frustration when nothing seemed to fit. I have had to practice not panicking, not giving up, but relaxing and accepting this frustration as a perfectly normal part of the writing process. I remember spending one Sunday largely staring at my computer, feeling exasperated and dying for a distraction. But I decided that maybe this was just my day for staring in exasperation and went with it, rather than fighting against it. The next morning I had a new burst of ideas and started rattling away at the keyboard.

Practicing a sense of ease can help foster new perspectives on complex problems. And it can help us interact in more fruitful ways. Sometimes, in a conversation or a meeting, we run into long, uncomfortable silences. The easy way out is to fill the gap ourselves. We want to do something. Say something. Change the subject or tell a joke to defuse the tension. But when we do this, we may lose an opportunity to really engage with a difficulty.

Having the confidence to wait and let the moment work itself out will often lead to something unexpected — and creative — happening.

∼

Play with reluctance

Despite our sparkling personalities and engaging wit and wisdom, it's often the case that the people we interact with would rather be elsewhere. Some don't want to be in the meeting or conversation at all. Others will drift off into their own thoughts for a while because they've become bored or annoyed. So how do we engage their attention in a fruitful way?

Simple solutions tend to be the most popular. We think that running an icebreaker will get everyone in a meeting focused together. Turning presentations into a TED talk will stop people getting bored.

Often, this kind of strained effort at engagement just annoys people and makes them more desperate to get away. Fake enthusiasm and feigned excitement can have big knock-on effects on the morale and effectiveness of an organisation.

There may be more wisdom in reflecting on what it's like to engage reluctantly as a participant rather than always maintaining the perspective of the leader. We've all struggled with paying attention to other people's presentations. It's useful to remind ourselves that this is what other people sometimes feel when they interact with us. Remembering our own reluctance can help us be a little softer and kinder when we encounter it in others. It can help us play with reluctance, rather than seeing it as an affront.

I sometimes start meetings with a line up, asking the participants to take a position according to how enthusiastic they feel about being here, in this room, right now. I invite them to stand at one end of the line if they're feeling wildly enthusiastic and at the other if they'd really rather be somewhere else, for whatever reason. A lot of the success of this exercise depends on setting up the line-up with enthusiasm and kindness, making any position sound interesting and legitimate. Most people feel negative about at least some of the meetings they go to, and that's ok.

I then suggest that people pair up with anyone else they like, from anywhere on the line, and have a chat about why they each chose their spots. They can share thoughts with a kindred spirit, or find someone with a different view, or just find out why a friend is in an unexpected position. You can often find energy and engagement just by being interested in where people actually are right now, instead of cajoling them to be somewhere else.

This kind of approach can be useful in all sorts of interactions. By being interested in dissent, reluctance, or downright refusal, we show interest in the reality of a person's feelings and engage with them directly. If we encourage people to conceal their reluctance, we don't get rid of it. It's still there, working away below the surface where it can be much harder to deal with. If we bring it to light, we will sometimes find that it can be a valuable resource.

∼

Seek difference

Unhurried conversations often go through a phase where everybody seems to agree. And then someone risks offering a different view. I've learnt to relish those moments, as for me this is when things come to life.

Not trying to force conformity is one important step we can take to help a diverse range of viewpoints flourish.

Difference is energising. When you gather diverse people together you multiply the possibilities for creating new cognitive connections. Many original ideas involve the combination of thoughts from very different perspectives. Exploring differences allows us to see things in ways they haven't been seen before.

By moving outside our own heads, we become able to create the sort of 'distant connections' that make creative breakthroughs possible.

Part Two: The unhurried path

Boredom. Gateway to the south!

In one of Peter Sellers' famous sketches, a trip to a drab London suburb is turned into a mock-epic adventure. An orchestra plays a soaring theme as the announcer booms, "Balham. Gateway to the south!"

Boredom might also be a gateway.

Sherry Turkle is an MIT professor who is fascinated by conversation. She sees the tricky, complicated and messy exchanges we normally consider to be obstacles as vital to making interactions work.[7]

> *Conversations, as they tend to play out in person, are messy—full of pauses and interruptions and topic changes and assorted awkwardness. But the messiness is what allows for true exchange. It gives participants the time—and, just as important, the permission—to think and react and glean insights. 'You can't always tell, in a conversation, when the interesting bit is going to come,' Turkle says. 'It's like dancing: slow, slow, quick-quick, slow. You know? It seems boring, but all of a sudden there's something, and whoa.'*

Dullness, in other words, is not only to be expected, it is to be celebrated. Some of the best parts of conversation are, as Turkle puts it, "the boring bits".

Being unhurried is not about using a secret technique to magically unlock answers to questions. It's about working with the natural flow of things. And part of this involves seeing that boredom is there for a reason. As the boring and mechanical features of our lives and work environments increasingly become automated, we face higher and higher cognitive loads on our brains as we lose more and more of the moments of mental downtime our thought processes rely on. But the more we seek to eliminate those moments and immerse ourselves in activity, the harder we make the acts of creative thought that those activities rely on.

Sometimes we can simply embrace those moments of boredom and difficulty, and see them as a resource.

Keith Sawyer's brilliant study of perceptions of creativity, *Group Genius*,[8] points in this direction. He cites research showing we easily confuse stimulation with creativity – people thought they were more creative on stressful, stimulating days and less creative on quiet, duller ones. The reverse turned out to be the case. We kid ourselves that we're more creative under stress, when the adrenaline is flowing and the pressure is on. But when looked at objectively, it seems that creativity is actually a much more ordinary process.

We're tempted by what I call the sugar-and-caffeine approach to creativity: lots of buzz and excitement and a conflation of high energy and stimulation with productivity. But in reality, that buzz is all just surface froth. At best, it obscures the processes going on at a deeper level; at worst, it leads to unnecessary stress and increased cognitive loads that can actually constrain creativity.

Alex Mayyasi describes research[9] on how much we really learn from apparently brilliant talks compared to the more normal dreary ones. Groups were shown two presentations, one a sparkling TED-esque talk in which the speaker was polished and exciting, and another with a speaker who droned through a reading from a prepared text. Unsurprisingly, the first was much more highly rated by the audience than the second. People thought they got a lot from it. But when researchers objectively measured what the audience had actually learned, there was very little difference in outcomes between the two speakers.

∼

Frustration is your friend

We all experience conversations in which people are just "talking or reloading." A satisfying interaction requires a different way of speaking to each other.

The theoretical physicist David Bohm advocated a type of dialogue in which all participants try to reach a consensus by taking full account of everyone else's views. Donald Factor, who worked with Bohm, had this to say on the importance of engaging with frustration:[10]

> *In my experience frustration is the one thing that is universal in a group's experience and this appears to also be the case in our entire culture… It could be argued that a great deal of our culture is dedicated to distracting us from our frustrations in an attempt at defusing them. The painful experience of frustration is, therefore, something that needs to be sustained in the dialogue so that its meaning can be displayed and understood. I have come to suspect that frustration may have to be seen as the crucial motivating force that can drive the dialogue deeper into unknown territory and thus toward the experience of creative insight.*

The idea that frustration might be the thing that holds a group together, something everyone can have in common, is counterintuitive but stimulating.

One of my favourite moments from years of attending psychotherapy groups was when someone shared how angry they were feeling with the group leader. Her response to this attack took me aback. She said, "I like anger. It can be so energising." We may instinctively want to run from anger, or to leap aggressively into it. A middle path of staying put, and seeing where it leads, can be a lot more creative.

∼

Learning is better than winning

Tim Gallwey, who wrote *The Inner Game* books,[11] once hosted a corporate tennis tournament for a client. Rather than set up a straight knockout contest, he decided to introduce a radical twist – the loser, rather than the winner, of each match would proceed to the next round. This approach overturned all convention and forced the participants to question what actually mattered about the game. What was the real purpose of this competition?

The executives taking part didn't reduce the tournament to a silly pantomime of deliberate errors. They still did their best, but they were all able to play with a useful sense of detachment from the idea of competitive victory. And those players who were least strong received the greatest learning opportunities.

Gallwey shares many more such stories from his work, revealing again and again how learning happens when we relax our attention and loosen our attachment to success.

In my own world, helping people have difficult conversations has taught me that trying to win the argument usually only makes things worse. We get seduced into a point-scoring mindset as a way to navigate through the tension of the moment and this only serves to escalate the conflict. Funnily enough, when we try less hard to win, we're far more likely to make the breakthroughs that will get us past the fight.

Many of the games I use in training sessions can be played ruthlessly to "win" or more collaboratively. In these improv games, the win is essentially trivial. This raises interesting questions about why many of us default to working so ruthlessly to achieve a meaningless victory, as well as questions about what it's really like to win. Winning can often feel quite isolating for the victor. It also ends the game and the exploration that goes with playing. On the other hand, failure can feel more connecting: we all recognise and feel attuned to a shared struggle and the possibility of getting things wrong.

I sometimes ask participants, "What if instead of focusing on 'winning' the current game, we look for ways to keep the game open and see what we can learn from it?"

This focus on learning rather than winning encourages us to lean into difficulties and see what can be gained from them, rather than rushing to dismiss or disarm them. When meetings or conversations fixate on getting through the agenda, this becomes another kind of attempt to "win". If we allow the time and space for more reflective processes, we tend to create and develop more useful ideas about the issue at hand. These approaches can help to change perspectives on what the group wants to achieve – and this willingness to consider new perspectives often leads to much wiser action.

∼

Getting over ourselves

I was the typical skinny kid who was always picked last for any team activity. Physical education mostly taught me that sport and humiliation were much the same thing.

I've spent my adult life gradually discovering the benefits of exercise, despite my experience at school.

But one thing has always puzzled me. I'd go to the gym and see these classes going on where people got breathless as they were shouted at by an over-enthusiastic trainer. Why would anyone pay money for that?

When I signed up for "Core Experience" at a local yoga studio, that sounded much more like my thing – slow focused exercise. It was going to be like yoga with a focus on the core. Great.

So imagine my horror at finding myself in a room of people doing an incredibly sweaty aerobic warm up, led by Karim Niangane, an impossibly enthusiastic Frenchman. Turns out Core Experience was the embodiment of the kind of vigorous class I despised. And here I was in the middle of it.

I hated every minute of it. I looked at the clock and thought, I can't do an hour of this! I stared at the clock, at the vast amount of remaining time and decided I would simply leave.

Yet for some reason, possibly the imagined walk-of-shame in leaving this tribe of fanatics, I stuck it out, second by humiliating minute.

Until, at some point, I started to inwardly laugh at the sheer absurdity of the position I'd put myself in.

I didn't convert much fat to energy in that first class. But a little bit of stubbornness did begin to turn towards enthusiasm.

And in the uncomfortable process, I realised I could let go of a story that ultimately wasn't about fitness classes, but was really about me. I found myself signing up for the next class and now I'm a bit of a fanatic.

Sometimes, we just have to let go of these old ideas of ourselves. Here's how psychoanalyst Otto Rank put it:

> *In the process of adaptation, man persistently separates from his old self or at least from those segments of his old self that are now outlived. Like a child who has outgrown a toy he discards the old parts of himself for which he has no further use ... the ego continually breaks away from its worn-out parts, which were of value in the past but have no value in the present.*

Unlearning and breaking from the past is at the heart of discovery and creativity. It is only when we can set aside old ways of doing things, old frames of thought and approaches, that we can really open ourselves up to new possibilities. As Rank observes, great artists like Rembrandt and Picasso were able to leave behind era-defining successes and move beyond old ideas of themselves to develop entirely new ways of reshaping the world once again.

Finding ways to move on from our successes is just as important as being able to move on from our failures. In order to continue to learn, we need to lose our attachment to old versions of ourselves. That doesn't mean we have to consign our identities to the void but if we can shake off some of the attachment we feel we can then explore the performance of other possibilities. By learning playfully, we can try out different versions of ourselves and bypass some of the stories our minds invent about us.

> *Do I contradict myself?*
> *Very well then, I contradict myself.*
> *I am large, I contain multitudes.*
>
> Walt Whitman, '*Song of Myself*'

For a long time, Western philosophy was hung up on the idea that every individual is a single soul with competing parts. The ultimate aim, according to generations of thinkers, was to get all these parts to stop fighting with each other and to bring them together into a single, unified whole. We now tend to recognise that this idea of psychological unity is a bit of a myth. We know that we don't have to be the same person at work and at home, in the meeting room and on the dance floor, and we generally accept that different situations call for different outlooks. But we still carry around the relics of the ancient view and find it hard to shake off the idea that this is all just surface level modification of the same underlying thing.

One of the easiest ways to deal with the complexity of the world is to embrace the idea that we are multiplicities and move beyond the notion that getting stuck in a single role is "authentic". When we accept that we can be a different person from moment to moment, we make it easier to flow with the complex whirl that surrounds us. People can act differently by changing their role. The old behaviours can be kept, hung up in the closet with the role and perspective they fit, ready to be picked up again when they are useful. By allowing ourselves to slide from one perspective to another, we avoid treating ourselves as problems that need to be fixed. When we feel forced to squeeze all these perspectives into a single truth, we get really stuck – when we allow them their own space, we give ourselves the ability to move.

∼

The spatula game and the teaching trance

The psychoanalyst Donald Winnicott noticed that if a mother placed a spatula near her child, and waited, it was very likely the child would become curious about this new object and play with it contentedly, exploring all its possibilities.

If, however, the mother joined in the play in an effort to teach something, the child was likely to do one of two things: they might reluctantly play along, developing a passive kind of engagement. Alternatively, they would react against this intrusion angrily.

Winnicott saw that angry response as the more healthy one.

We're so drawn to trying to teach and explain things to others, even to small children, that we easily fall into a trance that isn't good for relationships.

I call it a teaching trance. When you sit in any position of authority – that might mean you're the CEO, or perhaps you're the terrifying receptionist the CEO is scared of – the way you want things to be can define what success looks like for those working with you. Your views about how to do things can start to take on the aura of holy writ.

On the surface, as you dispense your wisdom, it can look like learning is really happening. People come to you and ask for guidance, giving you a status that sets you above others. This flatters the ego but it can also give comfort to those who look up to you by reducing their own sense of responsibility for how they learn and develop.

These feelings can make it easy to fall into the teaching trance. When we become too comfortable with our position of authority, we can become attached to giving explanations and answers. In turn, the surprise of discovery, learning new ideas, and tapping into other resources can all come to seem like threats.

Stepping out of the teaching trance allows discovery, rather than information, to be at the heart of learning. As David Rock and Jeffery Schwartz say in their article, 'The Neuroscience of Leadership':[12]

> *For insights to be useful, they need to be generated from within, not given to individuals as conclusions … Human brains are so complex and individual that there is little point in trying to work out how another person ought to reorganize his or her thinking. It is far more effective and efficient to help others come to their own insights.*

By avoiding the trappings of expertise, a person in a leadership role makes themselves more vulnerable. But at the same time, they also create more power and agency for those they work with and for the organisation they lead.

∾

Create agency

A fascinating experiment conducted in Singapore[13] shows the positive effects that giving someone a sense of genuine agency can have. Elderly residents in a nursing home appeared to be in decline, failing a series of simple cognitive tests. But when they were asked to help redesign the décor of the building and to water the new plants that were included in the refit, both their cognitive abilities and their willpower shot up.

This experiment shows the power in giving people agency and helping them find solutions on their own. It's sometimes comforting to tell people what to do, and some groups may look as if they want you to set the rules for them and steer them forward. But it's often worth taking the risk of appearing less certain about our own views and more confident in the ability of others to figure things out for themselves. When leaders hold back their impulse to direct and control, they can unlock resources that would otherwise never be available to them.

Moments

A funny thing happened to me on the way home from the cinema.

I was cycling down Regent Street in Cambridge when two men staggered into the street in front of me. They were clearly several pints the wrong side of sober.

I rang my bell to let them know I was coming. A couple of seconds passed as this signal slowly penetrated their alcoholic blur. They stared at me, moved slightly to one side, and then hurled loud, angry words my way.

Foolishly, I found myself yelling back, "I was only trying to let you know I was there". But the tone was defensive and whiny, and I think they received this as, "get out of my way, you idiots". Which is probably what the bell had seemed to say to them too.

You know the feeling. The one you get when you realise you are escalating a situation that doesn't need escalation. Part of me knew I should shut up, keep riding and get out of there. Instead, and partly in deference to a red traffic light, I stopped.

One of the men stumbled towards me, got right up close and yelled at me, and my bell. But it wasn't my bell I suspected he was itching to punch.

I realised things could get nasty, and quickly.

The previous summer, some friends came to stay with me. They were mates from the world of improv theatre and we had a high old time, wandering around the city, enjoying the sun. We shared a mixture of games and stories from our experiences of using improv in the world of work.

We rented a church hall, did some improv singing and then I showed them a process I use when helping people in organisations have difficult conversations. It involves getting real world examples of challenging conversations and rapidly trying out dozens of different ways to have them. We get someone to play the antagonist and we give them the most provocative line of dialogue. And then we rapidly iterate loads of different ways of responding. To use the language of agile software development, we do rapid prototyping – but of behaviour, not of products. We see what we can learn by experimenting.

Towards the end of the session, my Finnish friend Jani was in the hot seat and announced that he wanted to try doing "four sorries". He meant he wanted to try out four different ways of saying "I'm sorry" to see what impact they would have on the conversation. His versions were all different and worked in different ways. And when others joined in we found lots more ways of saying, sorry. The game of Jani's four sorries had become Jani's forty sorries. Some sounded sarcastic or dishonest or passive aggressive and clearly made the situation worse. Others seemed, somehow, to reduce tensions, and finally one provoked the person playing the antagonist to climb down from the attack they had been running.

I might not always try forty versions of two words, but each time I run this process, people get lots of practice at trying different things out in high stakes conversations, and lots of experience witnessing what does and doesn't work.

I stared at the drunk, as he stared at me. I realised that I shouldn't have let things get this far. But here I was, in the here and now. I had to come up with something that worked or I was going to end up down on the ground with my bike on top of me.

There was no time to think it through, so I went on instinct. An instinct that had been built up last summer playing Jani's Forty Sorries.

I stared back at the drunk. I met his gaze full on but without aggression or fear. And said, as openly as I could: I'm sorry.

There was a brief pause. You could sense that he was a bit surprised by this and a moment passed where you could pretty much see his mind trying to make sense of this development.

And then he surprised me back.

He stuck his hand out, and he said, "I'm sorry."

Neither of us said what we were sorry for. That didn't matter.

I shook his hand, and we both laughed. I said something about it being good to enjoy a Friday night and pedalled off. He called after me to wish me happy bell-ringing.

It was one of those moments when everything suddenly feels very real, and time stops. You sense that anything could happen and that what you do is going to have a big impact. I suspect that life is actually a continuous stream of such moments but we miss most of them because we're distracted.

I had no idea playing games that summer how our little practice might pay off the following winter.

I've begun to pay more attention to these little epiphanies, including starting a podcast series in which people can share them.

∼

Practice

According to legend, the famed cellist Pablo Casals was asked, at the age of 93, why he continued to practice. He replied, "Because I think I'm noticing an improvement."

Thinking about the work we do as "practice" can be a useful way of understanding the layers involved in it. When we see our actions and decisions as a step on a journey, as experiments in a learning process, it's easier to resist the urge to use the labels of success and failure. Complex systems don't yield to simplistic categories: today's successes can set the stage for tomorrow's failure, just as the lessons we can learn when something doesn't go as planned can help us improve our approach in the future. If we can move beyond ideas of good and bad, we find that we have more freedom to think about what actually happened and to learn from it.

The spirit of practice crosses back and forth over the questionable boundary that we use to mark off the difference between work and the other parts of our life. I have increasingly come to believe that all of life is practice, if we choose to think of it that way.

This is not an invitation to say, "Oh well … anything goes!". A spirit of practice encourages us to reflect more, not less, on how to work effectively.

To navigate the world in all its complexity and to keep afloat on its ebbs and flows, we need to develop skills that are based in parts of our brains that aren't focused on information and analysis. John Wenger makes a great related point in his article on transformational learning:[14]

> *Research indicates that skills based in this part of the brain are best learned through motivation, practice and feedback, rather than simple transfer of information. In other words, things that involve the "F" word (feelings) require a transformational learning process. As Emotional Intelligence guru Daniel Goleman states, "A brief seminar won't help, and it can't be learned through a how-to manual".*

We learn this stuff by practicing ourselves and by watching others practice, not by being handed a kitbag of tools and techniques.

The writer and boatbuilder Antonio Dias offers some valuable reflections on what practice means. He makes the important point that practice is not simply doing the same thing again and again until you get good at it.[15]

> *Practice … is not practicing scales, doing calisthenics, or running through any sort of programmatic solution to the problem of "mastery." Practice becomes a place and a time dedicated to allowing improvisation to happen.*

This sense of "allowing" can be hard to grasp. There's something paradoxical about it, and it doesn't lend itself to prosaic explanation. I regularly find myself feeling my way through interactions or my understanding of a problem. Sure, there are times when I can just run a process, but there are others when I feel a pressure to "do something" and I don't know what that something is. I tend to sit with the anxiety until a moment comes when I'm able to let go and just "allow" things to unfold. It's at that point that calm descends and a decision presents itself. My hunch is that it is the allowing of uncertainty, the stepping into the complexity without a guide-rope, that is the key. The practice of being unhurried only really starts when I step beyond simple "problem-solution" thinking.

∽

Despondent yoga

I talk about unhurried a lot because I may be the one who most needs the practice.

Unhurried is about remembering that it's possible to step out of the melodrama I've made in my head, and engage with the subtler but more satisfying drama of what's really happening, moment by moment.

In the last year, I've started to do a little yoga at home each evening, for maybe 30 minutes. I've tried to make it a habit as it helps me to sleep later on. But it's not always easy to find the motivation. I remember one time recently when I was feeling pretty down after a tough day. The idea of doing yoga made me feel worse. I felt despondent.

And then I noticed this thought: I could simply do despondent yoga. I might do it a bit half-heartedly, but I would do it. And so I started, and for a few minutes I did the postures a bit wearily. And at some point, it all just felt natural and ok. By allowing for despondency, I'd been able to get past it.

Unhurried isn't an end state of bliss, but a way of travelling through the muddled territory we find ourselves in.

Start anywhere

Researchers of complexity point out that the smallest change in starting conditions can have dramatic impacts on the later development of the whole system.

This is a useful insight.

But sometimes we forget that **where we are now** is always a starting condition for whatever is to come.

So this is where we start from.

And we might as well start now.

Notes and Thanks

Thanks to Rob Paterson for the Thomas Cranmer story, and Anne McCrossan for getting me thinking about the value of a mesh. Also to Rob Poynton, Cathy Salit, John Wenger, Lee Ryan, Antonio Dias, Kay Scorah, David Matthew Prior, Farah Ismail, Daniel Knutson-Bradac, Jeanne Walker, Ally Finkel, Rebecca Kerner, Roland Harwood, Declan Elliott and Huw Sayer for links, encouragement, and general good vibes. Thanks to Antony Quinn for dropping the word unhurried into a conversation and then supporting me on the journey ever since, and to Viv McWaters for her mad decision to invite me to work with her in Sri Lanka and then a whole slew of other places since. Thanks to all those people who attended unhurried conversations with me over the years for so many wonderful stories and insights that inspired this book. Paul Scade has been a brilliant editor, helping me to refine and deepen my thinking. For all mistakes, blame me.

I have changed some names and minor details of context in one or two of the stories to protect the innocent.

Cover photo by Ferne Millen.

You can find our more about unhurried, the unhurried moments podcast, and resources for unhurried conversations at this website: unhurried.org

REFERENCES

1. https://www.amazon.co.uk/General-Theory-Love-Vintage/dp/0375709223
2. https://www.amazon.co.uk/Talk-Science-Conversation-Elizabeth-Stokoe/dp/1472140842
3. https://www.amazon.co.uk/Logic-Failure-Recognizing-Avoiding-Situations/dp/0201479486/
4. https://www.ted.com/talks/manuel_lima_a_visual_history_of_human_knowledge
5. https://www.amazon.co.uk/Liars-Poker-author-Short-Hodder/dp/0340839961/ref=sr_1_1
6. https://www.spring.org.uk/2009/08/why-groups-fail-to-share-information-effectively.php
7. https://www.theatlantic.com/magazine/archive/2014/01/the-eavesdropper/355727/
8. https://www.amazon.co.uk/Group-Genius-Creative-Power-Collaboration/dp/0465071937/
9. https://priceonomics.com/is-this-why-ted-talks-seem-so-convincing/
10. http://www.david-bohm.net/dialogue/facilitation_purpose.html
11. http://theinnergame.com/inner-game-books/
12. https://www.strategy-business.com/article/06207?gko=f1af3
13. https://www.youtube.com/watch?v=WnTz8XXY9is
14. https://medium.com/@johnqshift/transformational-learning-3deb1bb2e865#.r11rlpbon
15. https://concentricdialogue.wordpress.com/2014/03/27/a-question-of-practice/

Printed in Great Britain
by Amazon